ANIMALS

Bears

by Kevin J. Holmes

Content Consultant:
G. Michael Schenck
Past President/CEO
North American Bear Society

Bridgestone Books
an imprint of Capstone Press

Bridgestone Books are published by Capstone Press
818 North Willow Street, Mankato, Minnesota 56001
http://www.capstone-press.com

Library of Congress Cataloging-in-Publication Data
Holmes, Kevin J.
    Bears/by Kevin J. Holmes.
    p. cm.--(Animals)
    Includes bibliographical references and index.
    Summary: An introduction to bears' physical characteristics, habits, prey, and relationships
to human beings.
    ISBN 1-56065-741-3
    1. Bears--Juvenile literature. [1. Bears.] I. Title. II. Series: Holmes, Kevin J.   Animals.
QL737.C27H65   1998
599.78--dc21

                                                    97-41713
                                                      CIP
                                                       AC

Editorial Credits:
Editor, Martha E. Hillman; cover design, Timothy Halldin; photo research, Michelle L. Norstad

Photo Credits:
Dembinsky Photo Assoc. Inc./Mark J. Thomas 12, 18
Cheryl A. Ertelt, 10
William B. Folsom, 20
International Stock/Mark Newman, 16
William Muñoz, 6
Root Resources/Alan G. Nelson, cover
James P. Rowan, 8, 14
Visuals Unlimited/Tom J. Ulrich, 4

Table of Contents

Ears

Eyes

Paws

Legs

Fast Facts

Kinds: There are eight kinds of bears. They include North American black bears, Asian black bears, polar bears, and brown bears. They also include sun bears, sloth bears, Andean bears, and giant pandas.

Range: Bears live in North America, South America, Europe, and Asia. Polar bears live on ice fields off far northern coasts.

Habitat: Some bears live in forests. Others live on mountains, plains, or ice fields.

Food: Bears are omnivores. An omnivore is an animal that eats both plants and meat.

Mating: Most bears mate during spring and summer. Some bears can mate anytime.

Young: Young bears are called cubs. Most cubs are born during winter.

Bears

Bears are mammals. A mammal is a warm-blooded animal with a backbone. Warm-blooded means that an animal's body heat stays the same. Its body heat does not change with the outside weather.

Adult mammals give birth to live young. Young mammals drink their mothers' milk.

Bears live all over the world. Four kinds of bears live mostly in northern areas. These are North American black bears, Asian black bears, polar bears, and brown bears. Brown bears are sometimes called grizzly bears.

Northern bears are large. Most hibernate during the winter. Hibernate means to spend the winter in a deep sleep.

Four kinds of bears live mostly in southern areas. Southern bears include sun bears, sloth bears, Andean bears, and giant pandas. These bears are smaller. They usually do not hibernate.

Sloth bears live in southern Asia.

Appearance

Most bears have large, round heads. They have round, furry ears. They have long noses. Most bears also have short tails and large paws.

Some bears have short hair. Other bears have long hair. Their hair can be white, cream, brown, gray, or black.

Some bears have markings. Andean bears are sometimes called spectacled bears. They are black with white fur around their eyes. The white fur looks like spectacles. Spectacles are eyeglasses.

The smallest kind of bear is the sun bear. An adult sun bear weighs between 60 and 143 pounds (27 and 65 kilograms).

The largest kind of bear is the polar bear. An adult polar bear can be 12 feet (3.7 meters) tall. It can weigh 1,800 pounds (810 kilograms). This is as heavy as some cars.

Spectacled bears are black with white fur around their eyes.

Homes

Bears live in North America, South America, Europe, and Asia. Polar bears live on ice fields off far northern coasts.

North American black bears spend most of their lives in forests. Brown bears usually live in open areas like meadows and valleys. Some brown bears live in forests. Sun bears live in the rain forests of southeast Asia.

Each bear has its own home range. A home range is an area where a bear lives and hunts. Bears mark their home ranges. They scratch tree trunks and leave scents. Other bears see and smell these marks. They know other bears live and hunt in these areas.

Most northern bears move into homes called dens during the winter. The dens are quiet and well-hidden. They hibernate in their dens during most of the winter.

Some brown bears live in forests.

Food

Bears are omnivores. An omnivore is an animal that eats both plants and meat.

Polar bears hunt and eat seals and walruses. Andean and sun bears eat honey, fruit, and insects. Sloth bears eat termites, ants, honey, and fruit. Giant pandas eat mostly bamboo. Bamboo is a tall grass.

North American and Asian black bears eat many kinds of plants. They eat berries and other fruits. Black bears also eat insects, frogs, and fish. Sometimes they eat animals that are sick, hurt, or young.

Brown bears eat berries and plants. Brown bears also catch salmon. Once a year, salmon swim upstream in some rivers. Brown bears catch and eat the salmon.

Bears that will hibernate need to eat large amounts of food. They must eat enough to last the whole winter.

Brown bears catch and eat salmon.

Skills

Bears have a good sense of smell. They can smell prey that is far away. Prey is an animal hunted by another animal for food. Bears can smell prey that is 20 miles (32 kilometers) away from them.

Bears are predators. A predator is an animal that hunts and eats other animals. Predators must see well to catch prey. Bears have good eyesight. They can see small movements that are 300 feet (91 meters) from them.

Bears can move quickly. North American black bears can run 30 miles (48 kilometers) an hour. Some brown bears can run 40 miles (64 kilometers) an hour. But bears can run fast only for a short time.

Most bears can climb trees. Sun bears often rest in trees during the day. Other bears climb trees to find food such as fruit. Some cubs climb trees to stay safe from enemies.

Bears also swim well. Polar bears can swim underwater for more than two minutes.

Sun bears often rest in trees during the day.

Mating and Young Bears

Adult male bears spend most of their lives alone. They find females during mating season. Mate means to join together to produce young. Bears usually mate in spring or summer.

Northern bears give birth to cubs during the winter while hibernating. Some southern bears also give birth to cubs in the winter. Others can give birth at any time during the year.

Female bears usually have one to four cubs at a time. At birth, the cubs are very small. Brown bear cubs weigh only one pound (one half kilogram). Newborn cubs are blind and have soft, thin fur. They drink milk from their mothers' bodies.

Bear cubs stay with their mothers for up to four years. Then they leave to find their own home ranges.

Bear cubs stay with their mothers for up to four years.

Polar Bears

Some polar bears live on ice fields near the North Pole. Many polar bears live on ice fields off the coasts of North America, Europe, and Asia.

Camouflage helps polar bears hunt. Camouflage is coloring that makes something look like its surroundings. Polar bears' white fur matches the snow. This allows them to sneak up on prey.

Polar bears swim to find some prey. Sometimes their food is far away. Polar bears can swim 60 miles (96 kilometers) without stopping. They have thick layers of fat that keep them warm.

Polar bears hunt seals above water. Seals live underwater, but they need air to breathe. Seals breathe by poking their heads through holes in the ice. Polar bears wait near these holes. They try to catch the seals.

Some polar bears live on ice fields near the North Pole.

Bears and People

Many people respect bears. Some cultures believe bears have special powers. Some people in Asia use bear bones for medicine. Bears are an important part of some Native American religions.

People hurt bears by destroying their homes. Some people cut down the forests where sun bears live. Others destroy places where bamboo grows. Giant pandas need bamboo.

People sometimes hunt and kill bears. Some people hunt bears for their furs or other body parts. Asian black bears and giant pandas are endangered. Endangered means in danger of dying out.

Many governments have laws about hunting bears. Some people work to help bears. They try to save places where bears live.

Giant pandas need bamboo.

Hands On: Heartbeat

Bears lie still when they are hibernating. Their heartbeat slows down. You can measure how quickly your heart beats. This is called your pulse.

What You Need

A clock with a second hand

What You Do

1. Find your pulse. You can feel your pulse in your neck. Place two fingers in the middle of your throat. Move them over about one inch to the left. You will feel a steady beat. That is your pulse.
2. Count the number of beats in one minute. Watch the clock.
3. Run around for ten minutes. Find your pulse again. Count the number of beats in one minute. Watch the clock.

A bear's heart beats about eight times each minute during hibernation. Your heart beats 80 to 100 times each minute. It beats more quickly when you are active.

Words to Know

cub (CUB)—a young bear

endangered (en-DAYN-jurd)—in danger of dying out

hibernate (HYE-bur-nate)—to spend the winter in a deep sleep

home range (HOME RAYNJ)—an area where a bear lives and hunts

mammal (MAM-uhl)—a warm-blooded animal with a backbone

omnivore (OM-nuh-vor)—an animal that eats both plants and meat

predator (PRED-uh-tur)—an animal that hunts and eats other animals

prey (PRAY)—an animal that is hunted by another animal for food

Read More

Patent, Dorothy Hinshaw. *Looking at Bears*. New York: Holiday House, 1994.

Sterling, Ian. *Bears*. San Francisco: Sierra Club Books for Children, 1992.

Useful Addresses

Bear Watch
1472 Commercial Drive #201
Vancouver, British Columbia
Canada V5T 2J6

The Great Bear
   Foundation
PO Box 1289
Bozeman, MT 59715-1289

Internet Sites

The Cub Den
http://www.nature-net.com/bears/cubden.html

Everything About Pandas
http://www.cnd.org:8013/Contrib/pandas/

Index